Troubled Treasures: World Heritage Sites

Tāj Mahal

Cynthia Kennedy Henzel

ABDO Publishing Company

visit us at
www.abdopublishing.com

Published by ABDO Publishing Company, 8000 West 78th Street, Edina, Minnesota 55439.
Copyright © 2011 by Abdo Consulting Group, Inc. International copyrights reserved in all
countries. No part of this book may be reproduced in any form without written permission from the
publisher. The Checkerboard Library™ is a trademark and logo of ABDO Publishing Company.

Printed in the United States of America, North Mankato, Minnesota.
102010
012011

 PRINTED ON RECYCLED PAPER

Cover Photo: Alamy
Interior Photos: Alamy pp. 23, 26; Corbis pp. 5, 7; Getty Images pp. 13, 19, 25, 28–29;
    Jupiter Images p. 9; iStockphoto pp. 1, 4, 6, 10, 11, 14, 15, 16, 17

Series Coordinator: BreAnn Rumsch
Editors: Heidi M.D. Elston, BreAnn Rumsch
Art Direction & Cover Design: Neil Klinepier

Library of Congress Cataloging-in-Publication Data

Henzel, Cynthia Kennedy, 195
    _____ _____ _____edy Henzel.
    p. cm. -- (Troubled treasures : world heritage sites)
  Includes index.
   ISBN 978-1-61613-568-3
   1. Taj Mahal (Agra, India)--Juvenile literature. 2. Architecture, Mogul--India--Agra--Juvenile
literature. 3. World Heritage areas--India--Juvenile literature. 4. Agra (India)--Buildings, structures,
etc.--Juvenile literature. I. Title.
   NA6183.H46 2011
   726'.809542--dc22
                            2010021306

CONTENTS

A vision of paradise sits beside the Yamuna River in Āgra, India. There, a terrace rises from the riverbank. Inside a wall grows a garden. Many buildings rest there, too. This place is called the Tāj Mahal.

Shāh Jahān was the fifth emperor of the Mughal **dynasty**. He built the Tāj Mahal in the 1600s. The main feature of the Tāj Mahal is a tomb. Shāh Jahān buried his wife there.

The tomb is one of the most beautiful buildings in the world. The outside is covered with white marble. Like an ice palace, its color reflects the changing light. Sometimes the Tāj Mahal looks shimmering white. Other times, it appears blue or orange.

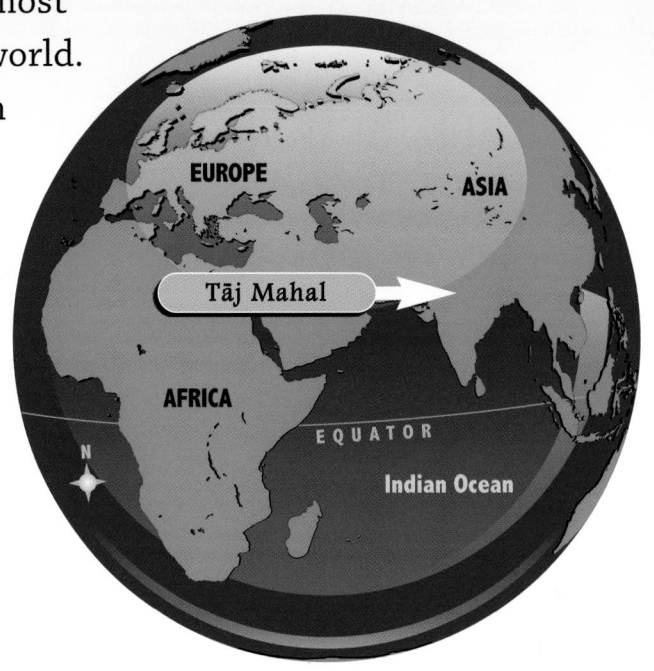

The Tāj Mahal is a majestic and powerful sight.

Tāj Mahal means "Crown Palace." It is the crown of the Mughal **dynasty**. This magnificent building is famous for the story of its creation. **UNESCO** officials recognized the worldwide importance of the Tāj Mahal by naming it a World Heritage site. This will help preserve this beautiful monument for years to come.

Humāyūn's tomb

The Mughal **dynasty** was founded by Bābur. In 1526, he conquered northern India. The kingdom eventually grew to cover much of India as well as Afghanistan and Pakistan.

The Mughals were **Muslims**. Yet, India was largely a nation of **Hindus**. As a result, the Mughals brought new ideas to India. These included tombs and elaborate gardens.

When Bābur died in 1530, he was buried in a garden. There, his tomb is open to the sky. Bābur's son Humāyūn became the next emperor. Humāyūn died in 1556. His tomb is much different from his father's. It is a very grand building. It was the first Mughal tomb built with a **dome**.

The third Mughal emperor was Akbar. He appreciated art, and the Mughal style developed during his reign. Akbar died in 1605.

Akbar's tomb seems to be inspired by several styles. Like traditional **Muslim** tombs, his is open to the sky. Yet, the tomb is stacked high like a pyramid. And, it was the first to feature minarets on its gate. These tall towers became an important part of Mughal design.

Akbar's tomb

LOVE AND LOSS

Shāh Jahān was destined to become a great Mughal emperor. When he was just 15, he met a beautiful girl. Her name was Arjūmand Bānū Baygam. She was only 14. The two fell in love right away.

Shāh Jahān and Arjūmand did not marry immediately. But their love remained strong. Finally in 1612, they married. Shāh Jahān named his new wife Mumtāz Mahal. This means "Chosen One of the Palace."

In 1628, Shāh Jahān became emperor. During his reign, the Mughal empire experienced its greatest prosperity. Shāh Jahān and Mumtāz were very happy. They spent all their time together.

Sadly, tragedy struck in 1631. Shāh Jahān was traveling on a military campaign. Mumtāz was expecting their fourteenth child. Still, she came with him. A healthy daughter soon arrived. But Mumtāz did not survive.

More to Explore
Legend says Mumtāz's final words were to Shāh Jahān. She asked him to build her a tomb.

Shāh Jahān was overwhelmed with grief. He chose a place on the Yamuna River to build his wife's tomb. There, the Tāj Mahal would soon rise.

The Tāj Mahal was Shāh Jahān's vision of Mumtāz's house in paradise. The garden is the heart of this paradise on Earth.

The Tāj Mahal is more than a single tomb. It is actually a group of many buildings and a garden. These are surrounded by a large wall.

Three Tāj Mahal buildings feature Arabic writing. They are the great gate, the tomb, and the mosque.

The Tāj Mahal was built with a public area and a sacred area. The public area was once a market for merchants and craftsmen. Today, it is no longer part of the Tāj Mahal. Instead, it has become a crowded section of Āgra known as Tāj Ganj.

The great gate separates this public area from the sacred area. The gate marks the entrance to today's Tāj Mahal. An open area lies before the great gate. It marks the change from public to sacred space.

The great gate is about 75 feet (23 m) tall.

Workers covered the great gate with red sandstone and white marble. These colors held great meaning for **Muslims** and **Hindus**. Red represented royalty, and white represented purity. The white marble is **inlaid** with Arabic quotations from the Koran. For Muslims, this is an important holy book.

Inside the great gate grows the fertile Tāj Mahal garden. The Mughals modeled their gardens after the Koran's description of paradise. They divided the land into four equal parts. Each part was planted with trees and flowers. The Mughals also built a wall to surround the whole garden.

Water from the Yamuna River keeps the Tāj Mahal garden thriving. Channels and pipes move the water from the river to four canals. The canals run between the four sections of the garden. As the canals flow, they water the gardens.

The four canals meet in the middle of the garden. There lies a square pool. It is 64 feet (19.5 m) long on each side. Visitors can see the white tomb in its reflection. Fountains fill the pool and line the canals. Water flows from 53 fountains in all!

Early visitors wrote that many fruit trees grew in the garden. Historians also know that Mughals loved flowers such as roses, marigolds, and poppies. Yet, little else is known about what Shāh Jahān grew there.

More to Explore
The four canals in the garden represent the four rivers of life described in the Koran.

The *Tāj Mahal* garden covers 42 acres (17 ha) of land.

Many Muslims still use the mosque today.

At the end of the garden, the glimmering white tomb dominates the view. A red sandstone building with white marble **domes** sits on either side. Each building has a pool in front. The two structures mirror each other.

On the tomb's left side rests the mosque. **Muslims** wash in the pool out front before entering to pray. Inside, the mosque has several special features. Indents in the back wall show the direction to face when praying. The floor pattern even resembles prayer mats.

Opposite the mosque rests the guest house. This building was not used for prayer. Instead, it was probably used for large gatherings.

The tomb, the mosque, and the guest house stand on a sandstone terrace. Down by the riverfront, it forms a decorative wall. The terrace is about 364 feet (111 m) wide and 970 feet (295 m) long. It is nearly 29 feet (9 m) high.

A tower rises at each end of the terrace wall.

In the Tāj Mahal, white marble suggests importance. The more marble on a building, the more important it is.

On top of the sandstone terrace lies a marble platform. It is about 300 feet (91 m) long on each side and about 19 feet (6 m) high. At each corner, a marble minaret rises 138 feet (42 m) into the sky.

The white marble tomb sits at the center of the platform. It rises a total of 223 feet (68 m) into the air. Each side measures 186 feet (57 m) long.

Crowning the tomb is a large, onion-shaped **dome**. It is about 144 feet (44 m) tall. The dome is a hollow structure. Yet, it weighs 12,000 tons (10,900 t)! On top, a decorative gold rod rises about 30 feet (9 m).

To build the Tāj Mahal, workers followed a design called eight paradises. Inside, an eight-sided room stands at each of the four corners. Centered on each of the four main sides stands an open, rectangular hallway. These eight spaces represent the eight paradises. And, they all connect to the center of the tomb.

The Tāj Mahal features a double dome. The inner dome rises about 80 feet (24 m) to form the ceiling. The outer dome rises over it.

The center of the Tāj Mahal tomb is known as the tomb chamber. This space rises to the **domed** ceiling. Artists covered the walls with Arabic writing and hundreds of decorative flowers.

To make each flower, artists used a special method called *pietra dura*. First, they carved shapes into the wall. Then, they cut tiny gems to fit into the hollow shapes. These stones fit together so well there were no visible spaces between them.

To create the colorful flowers, craftsmen used numerous semiprecious stones. These included blue lapis lazuli, green jade, red jasper, yellow and striped marble, and brownish red agate. A single flower could be made of 100 stones!

Mumtāz Mahal's grave is marked by a solid stone block called a cenotaph. It rests in the middle of the chamber. Artists decorated it with beautiful stone flowers and Arabic words from the Koran. Metalworkers crafted a gold screen to place around it. This screen was later replaced with one of carved marble.

The pietra dura *flowers have been restored frequently.*

A Labor of Love

Shāh Jahān ordered work to begin on the Tāj Mahal in 1632. After planning out the site, workers laid the underground pipes that would feed the canals.

Then, workers dug deep wells in the ground. They filled the wells with dirt, rocks, and cement. These solid foundations helped keep the terrace level.

Local workers made millions of small bricks for constructing the Tāj Mahal. These bricks were all made around the same size. Each is about seven inches (18 cm) long and five inches (13 cm) wide. And, each brick is about one inch (2.5 cm) thick.

More valuable stones were used to cover the bricks. The red sandstone came from about 28 miles (45 km) away. The white marble was brought about 250 miles (400 km). The marble slabs were very heavy. They were often cut 15 to 18 inches (38 to 46 cm) thick! At the site, metal rods and clamps were used to hold the stones together.

It took nearly 12 years and about 20,000 workers to build the massive tomb. Craftsmen continued decorative work for five more years. And, workers constructed other buildings until 1653.

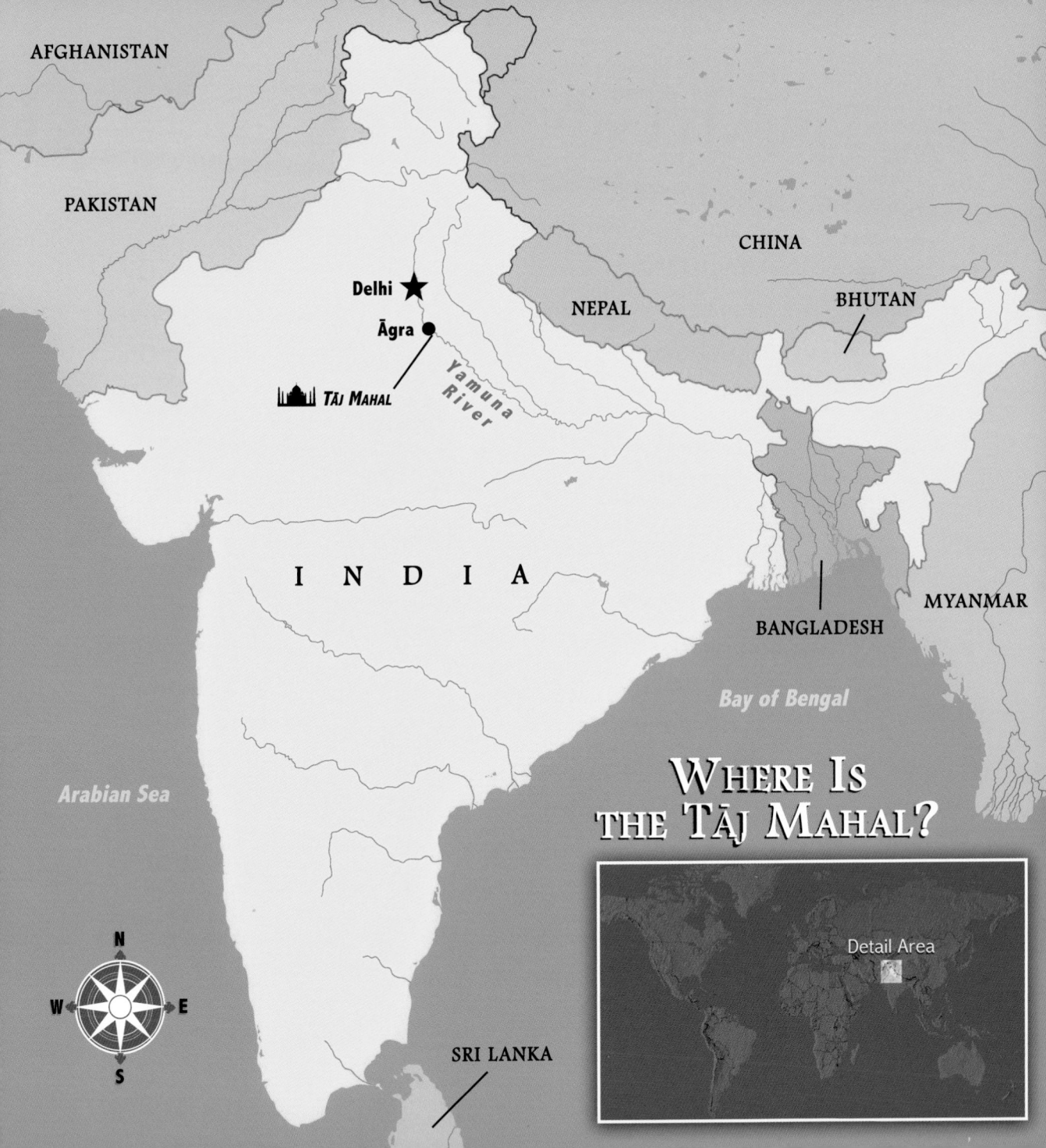

AFGHANISTAN

PAKISTAN

CHINA

NEPAL

BHUTAN

Delhi ★

Āgra ●

🕌 *Tāj Mahal*

Yamuna River

MYANMAR

BANGLADESH

I N D I A

Arabian Sea

Bay of Bengal

WHERE IS THE TĀJ MAHAL?

Detail Area

N

W E

S

SRI LANKA

In 1633, Shāh Jahān buried Mumtāz Mahal at the site of the tomb. Her grave lies in an underground burial chamber. Above it, her cenotaph points north. Construction had just begun the previous year, so work continued on the Tāj Mahal.

When the tomb was completed in 1643, people gathered to honor Mumtāz. Some chanted prayers beneath the **dome**. The shape of the dome held sound well. So, their voices sounded as if they rose to paradise. A single note could be heard for almost 30 seconds before it floated away!

Shāh Jahān continued to visit Mumtāz's tomb for many years. Then in 1648, he moved from Āgra to Delhi, India. He visited the tomb just once more in 1654.

Four years later, Shāh Jahān's son Aurangzeb seized the throne. Aurangzeb imprisoned his father in Āgra Fort. From there, Shāh Jahān gazed at the Tāj Mahal until his death in 1666.

Aurangzeb decided to bury his father at the Tāj Mahal. He had a beautiful cenotaph built and placed next to Mumtāz's. There, Shāh Jahān rests beside his true love.

Mumtāz's cenotaph (right) is
perfectly centered in the tomb.
Shāh Jahān's (left) is the only
element out of balance.

PROTECTING PARADISE

Shāh Jahān had arranged enough money to maintain the Tāj Mahal for many years. Aurangzeb saw to the monument's care during his reign. But by the late 1700s, many of the buildings were becoming damaged.

Then, the fate of the Tāj Mahal changed. Āgra fell under British rule in 1803. The British wanted to preserve several Indian monuments, including the Tāj Mahal. So, British workers cleaned and repaired the tomb. They even restored some of the precious **inlay** work.

In 1860, the British government founded the Archaeological Survey of India. This organization still maintains and protects the Tāj Mahal today.

Then in the late 1800s, Lord George Curzon was **viceroy** of India. He took an interest in the Tāj Mahal and began another British restoration project. Curzon rebuilt many of the buildings and replanted the garden.

More to Explore
Lord Curzon had a bronze lamp made for the tomb chamber. It hangs there today.

Indian craftsmen work to restore the beauty of the Tāj Mahal.

To protect the marble inside the tomb, visitors wear protective coverings on their feet.

Today, protecting the Tāj Mahal is no small task. About 7 million people visit the monument each year. Their footsteps wear down the sandstone walkways and marble floors. Crowds also increase the amount of moisture inside the buildings. This can damage the stone. Careless visitors even **vandalize** the buildings.

In addition to tourists, locals also threaten the Tāj Mahal. Nearly 2 million people live in Āgra. Cars and factories there add to pollution in the area. This pollution can create **acid rain**. When it settles, the acid slowly breaks down the stone. It also discolors the white marble.

In 1996, the Indian government ordered measures to control pollution in Āgra. Factories were told to close. Shops within the Tāj Mahal's walls were shut down. It also became illegal to drive cars near the monument. Visitors must now use other methods to travel nearby.

Unfortunately, these efforts have not eliminated the threats to India's monument to love. Pollution remains a serious problem in Āgra today.

A Monument to Love

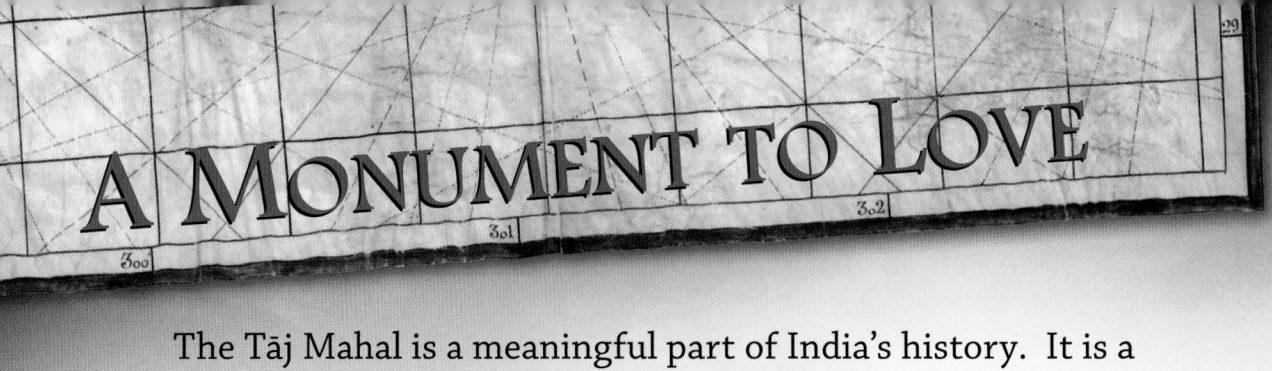

The Tāj Mahal is a meaningful part of India's history. It is a wonderful symbol of eternal love. And, it represents the power of the Mughal **dynasty**. It is the finest Mughal structure ever built.

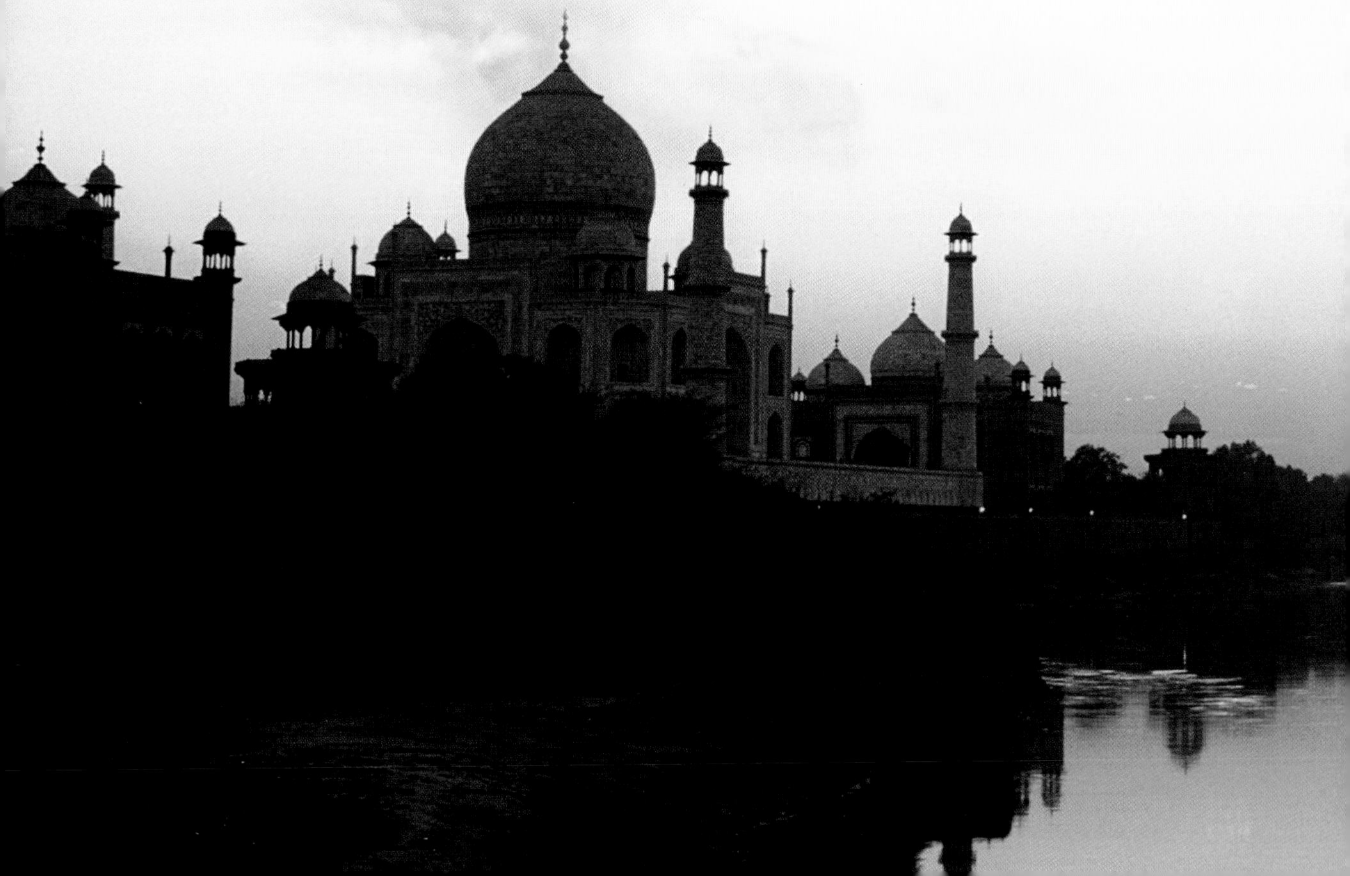

In 1983, **UNESCO** officials recognized the need to protect the Tāj Mahal for future generations. So, they named the monument a World Heritage site.

Meanwhile, scientists have been searching for ways to preserve the Tāj Mahal. They hope to find a coating that will protect the marble.

For now, they are using a new method of cleaning the beautiful stone. In 2008, workers covered the marble with a special clay formula. When the clay began to dry, the workers peeled it away. This treatment gently removed stains and dirt from the stone.

Mumtāz Mahal was well known for her great beauty. Today, the beauty of the Tāj Mahal is even more famous. With care, this treasure will continue to impress visitors for many years.

Our Valuable World Heritage

Around the globe, UNESCO World Heritage sites represent important civilizations and natural places. Cultural sites include historic buildings, towns, and monuments as well as important archaeological sites. Natural sites contain rare species or natural marvels. Or, they provide important examples of Earth's natural processes. Mixed sites share both cultural and natural elements. World Heritage sites protect and promote these global treasures for future generations.

GLOSSARY

acid rain - rain, sleet, or snow containing high amounts of certain acids. Acid rain is often caused by air pollution.

dome - a large rounded roof or ceiling.

dynasty - a series of rulers who belong to the same family.

Hindu - a person who follows Hinduism. Hinduism is a religion of India. It emphasizes rituals, ceremonies, and beliefs relating to correct behavior.

inlay - to set into a surface for decoration.

Muslim - a person who follows Islam. Islam is the religion of Muslims as described in the Koran. It is based on the teachings of the god Allah through the Prophet Muhammad.

UNESCO - United Nations Educational, Scientific, and Cultural Organization. A special office created by the United Nations in 1945. It aims to promote international cooperation in education, science, and culture.

vandalize - to intentionally damage public or private property.

viceroy - a governor who acts as the representative of a king or a queen.

SAYING IT

Afghanistan - af-GA-nuh-stan
Āgra - AH-gruh
Akbar - AK-buhr
Arjūmand Bānū Baygam -
    ahr-ju-MAHND bah-NU beye-GAHM
Aurangzeb - ahr-ang-ZAYB
Bābur - BAH-bur
cenotaph - SEH-nuh-taf
Delhi - DEH-lee
Humāyūn - hu-MAH-yun

Koran - kuh-RAN
mosque - MAHSK
Mughal - MOO-guhl
Mumtāz Mahal - mum-TAHZ mah-hahl
Pakistan - PA-kih-stan
pietra dura - pee-ay-truh DUR-uh
Shāh Jahān - SHAH juh-HAHN
Tāj Mahal - TAHZH mah-hahl
viceroy - VICE-roy
Yamuna River - YUH-muh-nuh RIH-vuhr

WEB SITES

To learn more about the Tāj Mahal, visit
ABDO Publishing Company online. Web sites about the Tāj Mahal are
featured on our Book Links page. These links are routinely monitored
and updated to provide the most current information available.
www.abdopublishing.com

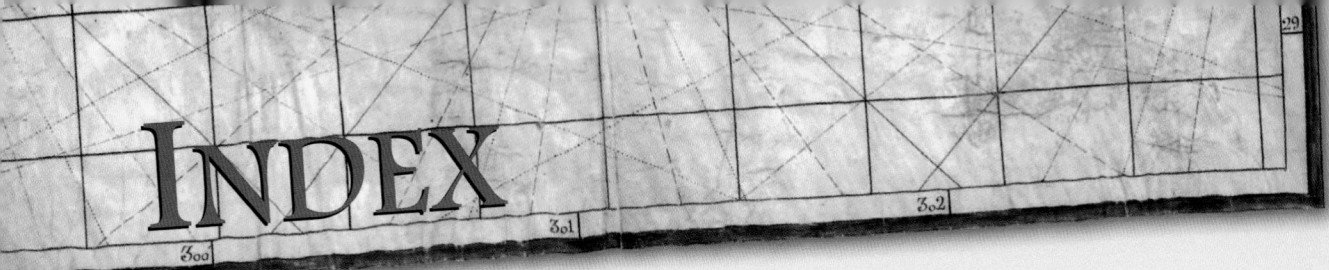

INDEX